Occult Church Exposed: My Firsthand Testimony

My Firsthand Testimony

Thabang Tefo

Published by Thabang Tefo, 2023.

OCCULT CHURCH EXPOSED: MY FIRSTHAND TESTIMONY

First edition. March 4, 2023.

Copyright © 2023 Thabang Tefo.

ISBN: 979-8215100295

Written by Thabang Tefo.

Also by Thabang Tefo

My Firsthand Testimony

Occult Church Exposed: My Firsthand Testimony

Power of psalms

Power of Psalm 144: Spiritual Warfare Deliverance Prayer for Healing and Breakthroughs!

Power of Psalm 23: Spiritual Warfare Deliverance Prayers for Healing and Breakthroughs!

Power of Psalm 2: Arrows That Destroys Bands of Wickedness

Standalone

Power of Psalm 1

Deliverance Prayers For Schizophrenia

The ABC of Prophets: Prophetic Guide Manual

Absence Of Fear: Guide To Fearless Living Through The Word Of God

Children's Bread: Practical Deliverance Manual From Demons

Occulthood In Church: My Firsthand Testimony

Table of Contents

Dedicated to friends and family.

Preface

Hi there. Thank you so much for taking your precious time to read this book. This is a profound and intense book that will leave many breathless, or even angry. I had to write this book for my brothers and sisters out there to know the truth. I couldn't agree with Christ more, when he said truth shall set us free. It is a precious freedom that birth peace of mind knowing who you are in the Lord.

This is my personal testimony about Zion Christian Church and how it is misleading many to the pit of hell. And how I was almost drowning in the sea of occultic priests. The things that I talk about in this book are true and I have seen and experienced them. This is not one of those speculative or journalistic book—it is a spirit filled led book.

It was through the power of the spirit of the living God that I was able to tap into spirit dimensions to see like prophet Ezekiel and see mystery behind this church. This is the biggest church in South Africa folks. Many have come and go, testifying about this church for doubling with the powers of darkness. The truth of the Lord it is that light that will dispel darkness.

I have spent years and years receiving revelations, visions, prophetic words, and intense dreams about the foundation of ZCC Church, its leadership, its agenda and mission. Allow me to take you on the journey through my depressing experience. The joy of the Lord is our strength. A book like this cannot come out without threats, even death threats.

My heart is for innocent millions of members who follow religiously without questioning some of the things in ZCC arena. I believe it is the power of occult mind control that will lead even the elect astray. This is just a piece of work to let you know that the power is in the blood of the Lamb. If God is absent, the devil is present. If the holy spirit is absent, opposing spirit is present. If Christ is not in the picture, the possessor—Baal is.

I wrote this book in a simple mannerism of English language. I believe a message can come across easy with an act of simplicity. Cheers!

Chapter 1-My journey

It all started when I was doing grade 11. I got a prophesy from a Zionist prophet that I wouldn't make it at the end of the year if I don't surrender my life to church. I literally got disturbed. I started attending church and performing injunction(Ditaelo) but I wasn't a member yet. Although most of my family member including my parents are member of Zion Christian Church. It clicked to me that I had to be baptized to avoid failing at school. What surprised me is that my mother had also prophecies prior about my baptism.

From a tender age, I had low self-esteem about my identity. Most of the time I was depressed. I was a loner. The church made my personality even worse as the prophecy will always tell me to be alone as my friends and family are against me. I was surprised how prophet in the church will overemphasis witchcraft in almost every piece of message.

Prophecy is for edification, exhortation and encouraging (Corinthian 14:31). Most of the time prophecy in church lead me to fear over faith as the main theme is witchcraft in many instances. How some of my family don't want me to prosper in education, job, marriage etc.

The prophet will not tell me to have faith in God or in Jesus Christ, but will tell me to have faith in the leader of the church. How with the leader Barnabas impossible are possible and how powerful he is. I had battle in my mind and I was peace less on how a human being like me can protect my soul and my spirit. For a long haul I had spiritual warfare with this believe. Because from tender age I always knew that there is God who is the Father of all in heaven.

In my intuition I always had that believe of monotheism. The one God whom Abraham bowed to. Whom Moses had trusted. Whom the Lord Jesus Christ communed with. We as African we fail God mostly by exalting men of God to the God status quo. We elevate men and put the creator in background. Blessed is he who trust in the Lord. Cursed is he who put his trust in men. I felt compelled to read the bible as it capsulate the truth. I'm that individual who is curious about many things and earnest to know. The prophesy will tell me not to look for knowledge, in fact, disapprove my eagerness to know, especially matters relating to church or religion.

Knowledge is power. Especially the right information and beneficial one. King Solomon had a wisdom from God, although he didn't rest but quest for knowledge, wisdom and understanding. The word of God says in Hosea "People parish because of lack of knowledge". House is built upon wisdom, knowledge and understanding. The foundation of everything worthwhile is the truth. I believe that was just a way of protecting the cult. The church promote education but they don't want you to be educated too much. They limit you on certain things. At some point one of the prophet told me that the Lord of the church doesn't want me to be too much prosperous because I will then forget the church.

It then clicked to me that blessings from the ZCC church doesn't come from the heavenly father but from the church. It's all about church agenda. The God of the church this and that. Jesus Christ is practically absent in the lives of the Zion Christian member. Jesus Christ is sometimes preached by the priest who are educated. Most of so illiterate priest will bombard you with the church leadership history and miracles produced by church. It's a law for ZCC priest to read the bible but will often switches and link with the Bishop of the church. I was disappointed how my 10 years and more in the Zion Christian Church was nothing more theocratic but historic in their theology.

Dreams and visions are part of life of Zionist. Whereby we tend to have faith in them as they direct, guide and at some point rebukes. rebukes. I noted that in the church there's an undying link between the living and the dead. As they always say during Mpogo rituals that the song Mpogo which is the anthem of the church is a way of connecting the dead with the living for blessing, protection etc.

Deuteronomy 18:10 "there shall not be found among you any one that make his son or his daughter to pass through the fire, or his daughter to pass through the fire, or that useth divination, or an observer of times, or an enchanter, or witch, or a charmer, or a consulter with familiar spirits, or a wizard, or a necromancer".

It all started with dreams were a man of God will make appearances in dreams. As it is the costume of the church that it is luck if you see the leader of the church in your dreams. The Leader of the church, Barnabas will speak in dream giving message, prophecy or just a mere appearance. I will start to wonder and ponder their meanings and interpretations.

I will go to the elders for clarity and they will tell me I'm chosen. Unbeknown to me he was initiating me into the marine kingdom and later I will the sacrificial lamb to the strange gods. ZCC is the church that believes in water ritual purification as they say. This is all part and parcel of the marine world. Whereby a minister is given a rank and command in the water of how to manufacture healing and miracles in the church.

I will often see him near lakes, streams, rivers and mountains. sometimes going into the water. In this oceans this is where they keep and lock the destiny of many believers. Meetings are usually gathered there. The idea of holy water sprinkling at church entrances is to initiate one into the marine world. This is cult church of the family whereby they protecting their own shrine. That's why is only family who are selected as the precedes. This is pure occultism! Fortune telling, magic practices, Spiritism, or false religious cults and teachings. The church built upon the blood of innocent men and women. I was almost a victim!

Now the narratives have changed. Human blood sacrifices now are done spiritually. The spiritualist will inject a snake on your body to draw your blood spiritually. There a many lost souls in ZCC who are dead spiritually, meaning detached from their silver cord because of these rituals. These souls are dedicated to the demonic shrines! I had an open vision whereby I was taken in the spirit to see lost souls in Moriah and the foundation of the church whereby I have seen dead souls as a result of human blood sacrifices. The underworld of ZCC are lost souls of people scarified to their strange gods. The ancient goddess Moloch is at play. For he requires the blood sacrifices of children.

My stay in the ZCC produced nothing but a story to tell. Mostly members of the church will tell you that you are playing with fire if you talk about the secrets of the church. That's the thing, a church with secrets! There is nothing secretive about Christianity.

The foundation of the Christianity is Christ who is the chief cornerstone. The church is built upon the apostle and the prophets, there is nothing secretive there. But ZCC, will tell you that this is the secretive church. Priest will often tell the congregants that ZCC is independent. ZCC doesn't need help. Lack of Christology pains me the most. though it paints itself as a Christian church. Perhaps in theology it does need help.

This book is my personal testimony of how I was almost lost. This book is not to taunt the name of the church or bridling the Zion Movement. But to let those who have ears to hear. The purpose of this book is to let out the truth as it is. How sick and fed up I am with ZCC. This is a spiritual book that requires spiritual lenses. It's time for Zionist members to open their eyes.

Don't let your soul sink because of these cult priests! The amount of endless disturbing sexual abuse in the spirit with mystical beings is something I have tolerated for so long. Surely I wouldn't be the only victim. Thousands are experiencing spiritual husband/wife in churches due to cultist priests as this is the marine spirit movement. Not only mythical spirits that sleeps with men and women but he himself is empowered by sex. Sleeping with people in the spirit.

Chapter 2-How it all started

It all started in dreams whereby the leader of the church will appear in my dreams frequently. He will lay a hands on my head, give me tea to drink and advices sometimes. I will often tell people that I always see the Bishop of ZCC in my dreams, they will say I am blessed. Because he is often regarded as deity, Man-God.

The dream that started it all was when I saw him holding a gun and shot me in the head. I started having headaches and unbearable inching pain in my head. I then started hearing voices in my head. He will usually come at night to take me to places, some of them I don't even know. I also started astral projection, out of the body experiences.

I believe at that time he was having challenges with his church. He required a blood sacrifice. I was to be that sacrifice unfortunately. This day some sacrifices a done spiritually. Even this trend of pastors sleeping with member spiritually, is real. I also heard a testimony of a certain Bishop who was sleeping with his member spiritually in a day light in church.

These are some of the cruel things I used to experience. He will come at night to sleep with me spiritually. I believe his spiritual powers is empowered by sleeping with people spiritually. Especially if you come from bloodline of Queens and kings. Because in the ZCC church they high regard people from that line- they are esteemed in their church.

He will come at night in a changed form of animal in my village at night. He will be among the witches and wizard of my village. One thing that witches and wizard do, each will have a partner to sleep with, as it empowers them. He will tell me to never tell anyone about it. One thing I will advise Christians about is the power of the blood of Jesus. And to learn to do spiritual warfare, binding and loosing according to Mathew 18:18. Witches and wizard they bind the atmosphere with their evil spirit to rule their territory.

I had a revelation wherein I saw lot dead soul in Moriah. The spirit of the Lord told me that these are blood of innocent men and women whom the church was laid upon. At some point later, I also had a revelation of Goddess Molech, who requires child sacrifices. This cruel goddess is the ancient Goddess found in the bible.

Molech is presented in the Hebrew Bible as the god of human sacrifice, a common practice amongst the people of the surrounding nations. The authors of the Hebrew Bible purposefully personified the sacrifice to Molech and presented it in a way to dissuade people from the continuing practice of human sacrifice. The writers explain that this practice is abhorrent to Yahweh. It is noticed that there was no demand for the first-born specifically in the molech sacrifice.

Chapter 3-Sangomic spirits (Moya wa Bongaka)

The holy spirit doesn't need assistance. He himself is called the helper. The holy spirit is called the helper, teacher, guider and comforter. The book of John and act of the apostles introduces the works and functions of the holy spirit. There is no link between the holy spirit and spirit of ZCC. In contrast, the spirit of ZCC you have to do certain things in order to prophesy. This is the time where it should be; freely we have been given, freely we should give.

There are certain injunctions such as holy water (Meetse a sediba), Joko tea, and their own branded tea to undertake for the process of becoming the prophet. This cannot be regarded as a gift or grace from God because you take responsibility upon yourself to see that you prophesy. If you don't prophesy expects serious punishment from the leader of the church and ancestors. The spirit of the Lord abides within and come upon the believers as he wills. And also fellowship with the believers. You don't have to do unnecessary commands of heading to waterfalls, mountains and streams of rivers in order for you to prophesy. This is pure paganism and sangomic!

As the true believer in God and Jesus Christ, you don't initiate as a prophet or as a priest. Holy spirit is a gift from God to the body of Christ. Ephesians 4:11 says when he ascended he gave gifts to men, some apostle, prophet, teacher and evangelist. These are some of the gifts to the body of Christ. The holy spirit came upon the believers in the day of Pentecost as a gift from above. The apostle were endowed with power from above to do the works of the kingdom. I

regard the spirit of ZCC as the same as the sangomic spirit whereby you have a choice of which food to eat and drink. At some point you head to rivers and mountains for cleansing and water purification. I was even told specifically that I wouldn't prophecy if I don't go to the waterfalls. There is undeniable contrast contrast between the holy spirit and the spirit of the ZCC church.

Worship of Indian gods and goddess

At one point in life I had an open vision where I was asking the leader of the church why he prays to Indian gods such as Shiva. He told me specifically that we all pray to Shiva. That was then when I was a member. It is not some folk tale whereby you hear members of the church saying Bishop is a powerful, and dangerous man.

I contest it to true because Lord Shiva is the Lord of destruction. He is also called the Lord of the animals. I also had a vision where I saw the shrines of Indian deities in the ZCC. This is a revelation from God about who is the leader of the ZCC since his position seems to be a mystery to many. Pure deception. ZCC is an anti-Christ movement.

This is a deception because all ZCC members they don't know who they are praying and worshipping. They often talk about the God of Mount Zion but clearly ZCC is a polytheism church, not a monotheism like semantic religion such as Judaism, Christianity and Islam. It takes some of its roots from Hinduism and other ancient forbidden religious practices.

Zion Christian Church rules in the second heaven. There is a throne where the leader of the church sit on which has snake on each side. His powers stem from there. In regard to Shiva, he is always depicted holding a serpent. The colors of these snakes are blue and yellow. The holy city Moriah is guided and protected by these snakes. They roam around the church headquters. You have to be on your A game spiritually to see them.

Worship of animals & Mythical creatures (Spirit of the animals)

These mythical creatures are spirits animals that resides in the lakes, streams, Mountains and oceans. These are nature spirits that govern the atmosphere, atmosphere, earth and seas. Genesis 6 shows us where this fallen spirits comes from. They were once the ministering spirits of God. Since now they inhabit this world, they have resembled the nature of their residence. Those angels who fell on water took the forms of mermaids.

The idea of fetching holy water from mountain caves, lakes and fountains is a picture of paying homage to these spirits. This is what I used to do as instructed when I was a member of Zion Christian Church. The prophet of the church will even tell you to bow to the lake before fetching water and plead with the owners of the rivers to allow you to undertake and perform cleansing rituals. Same applies to mountain waters, before you can fetch you pay homage. Some even drop coin money in caves for bit of luck and protection.

Chapter 4-Second Heaven/ ZCC heavenly place (Mid heaven, second heaven)

Members of the church will practically and proudly say their ZCC rules even in the heavens. Unbeknown that there are different different kind of heavens. Even the literal atmosphere of blue sky is called heaven. In Genesis, the Lord God created heavens. (2 Corinthian 14) Apostle Paul narrate to us how he knew a man in Christ who was caught up in the third heaven. This clearly shows that there is the third heaven. And practically or logically, if there is a third heaven, then there must be first and second heaven.

Usually the ZCC prophet will say "Thus says the God of Mount Zion in the third heaven or Thus says the God of the church". It's common for the prophet to include the three names of the church leaders, Engenas, Edward and Barnabas. I have had numerous or countless out of body experiences, visions, trances and dreams whereby I was translated to their heaven. I found out that they rule in the second heaven! The second heaven is not the habitation of God and the holy angels.

Their heaven resembles much of what in Moriah near Thabakgone. Their own holy Jerusalem is there. I was surprised to see the earthly structures that aren't so appealing. There are no golden routes, throne, angels etc. The same way we living in this earth, is the same of the people I saw making ends meet there. They day by day go about the church agenda, praying, worshiping, and dancing Mpogo. Some of the people there weren't even happy to be there. Some had no food to eat.

At some point I was even confused thereof. To found the cow ruling in the heaven. It is common and traditional practices of the church member to call their leader by his totem animal "Kgomo" meaning Cow. The Jerusalem in the heaven of ZCC has the emblem of the cow. But not an ordinary cow, wild and vicious looking cow with horns. The dreadful red eyed looking cow that seems satanic. This is what I saw. It's a total deception when prophets say God of ZCC is speaking from the third heaven.

God of the ZCC does not resides in the third heaven but the second heaven where there are satanic hosts. Majority of the member don't know that the second heaven is ruled by the devil. The devil is an imitator of God. He was once the angel of light. Thus from time to time he disguises himself as the angel of light.

Marine Kingdom Throne & flying serpents (Meeting, world conferences etc.)

It is not fictional, that there are kingdoms, cities and life in the underworld kingdom. Usually meeting of the satanic kingdoms and the darkness movement are conjured up in the marine kingdom. The leader of the church has a throne in the underworld, and highly ranks among others. There's no witch, wizard or sangoma in South Africa who can go head to head with him. That is why the ZCC church is known for protecting its member from witchcraft. Witchcraft is kind of a trademark is ZCC and is widely practiced by some members. Most of the priest sermons will center around the theme of witchcraft.

The ideal lead is to instill fear in the lives of congregants to never ever think of leaving the church. The prophets of the church will bombard you with witchcraft prophesies to implant fear instead of faith in you. The ideal goal is to lure you to see their church as the only way, and as powerful. They will tell you to trust the leader and to put your faith in him. This is what I will typical call the man God. Similarly, to the ancient practices of King Pharaoh of Egypt and Nebuchadnezzar of Babylon as they were man God.

ZCC Bishop has spiritual powers in this marine kingdom. He can send witches and wizard to whoever wrongs him. He delegates and organize in the underworld. Even the strongest spiritualist in this world have nothing on him in terms of powers. The flying serpents he uses performs all the magic and miracles happening frequently in the ZCC church. It is widely known wherever he goes it rains. It is true, basically the flying snakes accompanies him wherever he goes. They make it rain! And also the presence of sacrificed souls of men and women. That's how powerful he is in the marine kingdom. And most of the strategies of healing illnesses and diseases are fabricated there.

Gods of Mountains (Mythical creatures)

The powers of the church come from multiple sources. This is what is typically called polytheism. Whereby the religious cult movement believes in multiple gods. Especially animalism because mountains contains different spirits animals. ZCC leader consult this mythical creature's spirits of the mountains. It is not by surprised that his headquters is the mountain, called Mount Moriah. The area was well known for its snakes. Mythical creatures such as snake, Mamolambo(serpent) or mmamogashwa are trademark of ZCC church. To prove this statement one has to diligently take a look at manifestation of ZCC prophets when they are in spirits. They move their hips and body too much because snake sit on hips, and snore, or hisses often. These are, but few signs of snake manifesting.

The holy spirits of our Lord Jesus Christ promised in the book of John is replaced by the power of snakes in the Zion Christian church movement. Water snakes, mountain snakes, desert snakes etc. are the prototype of the holy spirits in the church. The church has its foundation or origin from India. The flying serpents from Indian oceans is in control of the church. I was fortunate enough to be taken in spirits by the Lord to see the whole operation of the ZCC church. Particularly to witness how things are manipulated in the spirits world of the church.

The bible says God our Lord is highly exalted on the throne and around his throne are seraphim's and cherubim's (Isaiah 6). however, that's not the case in ZCC because they don't serve the God we serve as Christian community. The throne of ZCC is snakes on each side, and sitting on the throne is the leader who is seen as God merely by the members.

Every time a new member is initiated or what we call baptism of three immersions in the church, members are initiated by snakes in the waters. What we call marine spirits, dangerous spirits that resides in waters to control the life of the believers into their conformation. Marine spirits are highly wicked spirits resulting in poverty that doesn't want one to accomplish something tangible in life.

Snakes are poisonous animals. It's a venom that has the capacity to kill people once its penetrates into human flesh. Many members in the ZCC dream of snakes and they will say it's the dead spirits of your ancestors or their guidance. This is a deception! one can attest that dreaming about snakes gives room for difficulty and marital problems. Snakes are common dream symbol of marine terrible spirits and household foundations in the life of a believers.

The spiritual feature for snakes in the bible is demonic. Snakes can symbolize many negative symptoms. These includes hindrances, oppression, lack, untimely death, terrible afflictions etc. Satan represent snake in the spirit realm. It is a symbol of evil powers and attacks from the kingdom of darkness.

Snakes are associated with tragedy, disasters and symbolizes the need for temptation to wallow into sin. It started way in the garden of Eden to revelation as dragon. Ultimately the snake grew from Genesis to revelation. It is still the same snake that deceived people in the times of Noah, Abraham, Moses and Elijah. Remember the floods, Sodom and Gomorrah, Egyptians in the times of Moses, Babylon, Elijah with the Baal movement etc.

The serpent was craftier than any of the wild animals the Lord God made (Genesis 3:1). In some way, the serpent was used by Satan to lie to Eve and lead her into disobedience. Moreover, Satan spoke lies through the serpent to Eve, and ever since then the snake has been associated with sin and evil spirits.

That's why it is very bad for any Christian to experience the movement of snake in their lives. Marine spirits are the highest in rank in the kingdom of darkness. These spirits are huge reality plaguing and deceiving even the most elect in the body of Christ, especially in Africa. Like ZCC, they believe in water purification. Ministers use water to perform healing. The trademark of the kingdom of marine.

Chapter 5-The foundation of the church

The foundation of every Christian church is Christ, who is the rock of the church. The chief cornerstone! The holy scriptures say it was built upon the prophets and apostles. The saint peter is the first stone upon where the church of Jesus Christ is build. The apostolic movement started with the 12 apostle.

The roots and branch of David is the chief cornerstone wherein the apostle are the stones. The notion of the rock still emanates in the Zion Christian church. The Church leader is widely regarded by majority of his followers as Leswika (the Rock).

However, I had a shocking revelation from God that ZCC church was built upon the blood of innocent man and women. Human sacrifice has been its pillar for a long haul. I have been in the underworld of ZCC, I have observed the lost, wondering and hopeless souls of children, men and women.

I have seen the record of soul sacrificed and I was supposed to be next in line. It is by the grace of God I am still breathing. I spend my Christian life unhappy, life filled with guilt, shame and condemnation. The church is so controlling and dictating in all aspect of your life. While the word of God says there is no condemnation to those who are in Christ.

Witchcraft is when you imposing your power on individual to try to control their lives through supernatural means. The power to control, rule, dominate without the holy spirit, result in the works of the witchcraft. As I said earlier, holy spirit is absent in ZCC, however the dead spirit of ancestral worship. Holy spirit is the third personality of the idea of trinity. I personally regard the holy spirit as the spirit preceding from the throne of God.

The works of the holy spirit are clear: To teach, lead, guide, comfort etc. however, the opposite of the holy spirits works are evident. This will be the works of the flesh. Is where you attempt to exercise control over others for personal gain. Deliberate witchcraft would be practiced by someone in the occult or Satan worship. You don't have to be a witch or warlock to practice witchcraft. When we go to a witch to gain hidden knowledge or something for ourselves, we are seeking to them as we would seek to God. We are submitting ourselves to them, become obligated to them and they begin to exercise control over us.

Likewise, going to Zion Christian churches they are submitting under the Zion deities who will control their lives. Majority of work is manufactured through dreams. For instance, you will dream wearing their attires or participating in their function then automatically it will clink in your mind. Finally, will visit their premises. Marine spirits or water spirits under water fabricate this kind of dreams to initiate members.

How Soul ties are made.

If you went to a fortune teller to get your fortune told, then you formed a soul tie with that person. There will be an attempt to control your life by that person from then on. Attempted control forms a soul tie. Demons will be sent out to help you and to draw you back to the fortune teller. This happens when you're thinking of consulting the church for help through injunctions. You form a soul tie and it is a doorway for dreams and vision induced by the spirits in the injunctions. You might dream the bishop of the church afterwards.

What I have picked in the spirit is that the leader of the two church pay homage to Indian gods and goddess. Barnabas Lekganyane is a polytheist man but more than other deities he pays homage to Lord Shiva. Shiva is widely known and referred in Hinduism as the god of destruction. destruction. He is often depicted with a huge gigantic snake as he is called the Lord of the animals.

I have had countless of dreams and vision were I saw the throne of the church leader in both side there were snakes. The color of the snakes resembles church attire of blue and yellow. This is basically where the church attire of women comes from. However, there are stories in church that the founder of the church received the attire of the church from the angels.

Going back to soul ties, ties are formed through snakes. There is a huge snake with a big eye or third eye that controls the minds of the members and the spirit of prophecy within the premise of the church. Sometimes the leader sends snakes to members to control your mind. These snakes sit upon your head or forehead. They control your thoughts, mind and spirits. Some of the dreams and visions are induced by these snakes. They inject fear in the lives of members so that you will always fear him. Besides mind control snake's powers, he uses the power of branded holy tea, coffee and water as a point of connection.

Mind controlling spirits

The worst form of occult ritual abuse is that done by the Satanists who program the person to follow Satan all of their lives. This is the objective of this church, Zion Christian Church. They initiate their member to marine spirits, to be ruled and controlled by these spirits. I had a vision or rather I was in spirit whereby I saw a throne in the underworld of the Marine kingdom sitting on was Barnabas and his wife. His whole operation and powers stems from this dark kingdom. Jesus Christ is absent in the lives of Zion Christian Church members. It is a taboo to even call upon the name of Jesus, or even to pray in the name of Jesus.

This is high demonic order to the extent whereby humans are sacrificed to their goddess Molech. The ancient and cruel god who requires the sacrifice of human blood of babies. Traditionally, Traditionally, it was believed that Molech was a god requiring human sacrifice as part of his worship (Lev. 18:21; 20:2-5; 2 Kings 23:10; Jer. 32:35).

I had a vision wherein I was underworld in the arena of ZCC and I was given food to offer to the goddess named Molech. In that dream I refused. This shows you that goddess Molech is worshiped in Zion unknowingly. There were other instances members will miss during three festivals in Moriah. Some were found but others were not found even to this day.

Mind control is the big thing in the kingdom of Darkness. The enemy is after your mind. If he can capture the mind of the believers, half of his job is done. Whenever you encounter the bishop of ZCC in your dream laying hands on you, he is injecting the spirit of mind control. And the spirit of fear so that you will always be afraid of him. The spirit of mind control blinds the mind of the believers. It the black clouds covering your mind affecting your intellect, reasoning and emotions.

WITCHCRAFT ATTACKS IN SPIRITS

A person in the dark sciences can do soul travel into the victim's presence and put a fragment of their spirit into the victim's spirit. The purpose of the witch is to control the victim and force that person to do what they command. There would have to be an open door in the victim's spiritual armor for this to happen. It can be dealt with by cutting the silver cord which causes the witch to die or by forcing the witch to remove the fragment of their spirit from the victim's spirit.

The sorcerers and witches usually do these at night to their victims. You will start to experiment with dreams and visions inspired by these cult people. Unfortunately, if you lack the spirit of discerning you will be in a big problem. Dreams and visions are important to us as they communicate our heart and soul. God often uses these medium to communicate with his children. Thorough spiritual warfare is essential to dismantle these evil strongholds.

WITCHCRAFT ATTACKS IN DREAMS

Sleep is a war front of demonic manipulation and attacks. Attacks in dreams include witchcraft initiation curses, spells, arrows and fiery darts. Demonic prosecution may involve death or financial adversity. The man of God will utilize night times through dreams. Because he knows that we are vulnerable when we are asleep. He will use night times because the enemy has power in the darkness. I will often see myself in these demon infused dreams drinking and eating while with him. Sometimes he will sprinkle water as if he is cleansing me. This was all part and parcel of the initiation.

Chapter 6-Satan is after your mind

Mind control is the chief weapon of Satan to snare the believer. The Scriptures admonish us to bring every thought into captivity (II Cor. 10:5). Many times a person will enter a world of fantasy and imagination, lusting after something or somebody or of something they consider normal. This is a counterfeit for what we are supposed to do when these thoughts enter our minds.

I have listed this mind control because it the A list weapon of the enemy against the believer. I saw a vision whereby the Leader of Zion Christian Church uses the power of snakes to capture the mind of his member. It is a snake with a third red eye. Through it you will obey what he says. It sorts hypnotize and control the minds of the believers. I personally was the victim of this satanic tricks. He manoeuvres most of the times in dreams while asleep and he himself with put snakes on each on the forehead to capture and control your thoughts.

Necromancy

Ancestor worship is practiced in different forms around the world today, even in cultures participating in the modern global economy. Ancestral beliefs are deeply dependent on the premise that the souls of the dead may return to the living and influence their lives; that it is possible and acceptable for the living to communicate with the dead and lastly that the living are able to exert an effect on the destiny of deceased ancestors.

Undoubtedly, ZCC depend on these premise of ancestral veneration. ZCC leader assemble the spirits of the dead and communicate with them in many instances. For example, when he wants to enquire about the future of a certain member, likewise he will do so by calling the spirits of the dead relatively. Whenever he has a mass gathering(Thapelo) or meeting, he is accompanied by the spirits of the dead, water spirits, desert spirits and Mountain mythical creatures. it is widely known that where he goes it rains. It is mainly because of these creatures that he assembles whenever he has a gathering.

ZCC takes its roots from India. The flying serpent's that performs all these magic of rains, storms and disasters is the stronghold of the Zion Christian Church. The shrines of Indian gods and goddess such as Shiva, Krishna are the backbone of this mega church. They will use a bible as the standard base of the church nevertheless they deny the deity of Jesus Christ.

Individual who approaches ZCC for guidance and prophecy, are on a long haul contact with the dead souls. The Biblical account of Saul's visit to the Witch of Endor is an example of this. On this occasion, he sought out Samuel's dead spirit for guidance. The Bible strongly condemns such practices (1 Samuel 28). Yahweh abhors such practices because it denies Him as the Sovereign Creator and Living God. Leviticus 19:32 The Bible exhorts Christians not to consult the dead.

Spiritism is the notion that the living can communicate with the souls of the dead by means of mediums (individuals who act as intermediaries between the material and physical world). The Bible has a negative view of necromancy or attempts to communicate with the dead.

In fact, all contact with the spirit world is expressly forbidden irrespective of the nature of the spirits concerned (Leviticus 19:26-31; Deuteronomy 18:10-11; Job 7:7-10; Is 8:18-20; Luke 16:19-31). The church of ZCC is undeniably the church venerates or meditate between the living and the dead. The word of God is against the necromancer, one who communes with the spirits of the dead.

The God of Abraham, Isaac and Jacob is the God of the bible who is against necromancy, Divination, Sorceress or consulter with the familiar spirits. With this idea at hand, it is clear that the God of Abraham is not the same as the God of Engenas of Zion Christian Churches. Clearly the Abrahamic religion takes their stand of the idea of monotheism. The bible is not relevant in ZCC movement. It is just a way of Christianizing the church to fit the arena.

Prophet Isaiah call out that can a nation seek advices from the dead while the is a living God? That's a ZCC right there. The most painful part is that the church highly regards sangomas than Christians. Leviticus 19:26 commands: "Do not eat meat with the blood still in it. Do not practise divination or sorcery" (NIV). This Scripture has particular relevance. Therefore, the basic meaning is ritual and sacrificial: draining the blood onto the ground would nourish deities or spirits.

The overall meaning of Mpoho is to strengthen the spirits of the dead and the living. It is a commune between the living and the dead. This is a practical divination ritual because it involves the sacrificing of an animal on the ground rather than on a stone, draining the blood into a deep trench and allowing the blood to soak in before the meat of the sacrificial beast could be consumed. The significance of this blood rite was that it is believed to draw the spirits to the surface and that it enhanced their powers of foretelling future events.

Majority of songs pay homage to the Bishop. Symbol of cow is centric to most of the worship songs. Most of Indian rituals requires requires slaughtering of cows. Cow is utmost important in the Zion arena whereby even the gathering in homestead called Mpogo take on cow slaughtering. Songs that praises Jesus Christ are just for the universal branding as it is called a Christian church. The leader is highly esteemed more than Jesus Christ or rather more than God. The name of Jesus Christ is hardly to find in ZCC. Even on pulpit majority of priests don't mention the name of Jesus. Engenas has substituted the name of Jesus Christ.

The theme that is going around is the idea of connecting you with your dead relatives for protection and blessings. That is why songs such as Mpogo a so centric to the church. We were told that Mpogo is the foundation of the church. It is pretty clear from this point that Christ is not the chief cornerstone or the foundation of the church. Because they talk about Badimo more than they talk about Christ. Even in prophesy Christ is rarely mentioned. The three leaders from different times, Barnabas, Edward and Engenas are mentioned.

This notion reminds me of the ancient kings and queens of Egypt who were worshipped. The Pharaohs of Egypt were gods to their people. People worked so hard to their kingdom. They had to pay tithe to their empire from difference sources, especially in agriculture as it was trademark of those times. There a thousands of ZCC members in Moriah who a laboring day and night for protection and blessing. Some of them spend more than 20 years working there without a pay. It is painful because these are our brothers and sisters.

Sexual dreams with mystical creatures are common. Especially in African initiated Christian churches majority of believers are experiencing spiritual wife/husband. As ex member of the church, I used to find most brothers in caves, mountains and lakes performing injunctions of dispelling spiritual wives. To my best of knowledge, also as a victim, it is hard to disperse a spiritual wife out of your life. For it is a covenant to be broken that requires raising an alter in place.

I have spent almost 10 years of my life struggling with spiritual wife. Only to found later that I was initiated into the marine kingdom! I did almost what can be done but to no avail. The only full deliverance one can receive is through the Lord Jesus Christ. By repenting and accepting the Lord Jesus Christ as the Lord and savior. For a long time, I didn't know that Barnabas was behind the scene as the marine spirits disperser and controller. Thank God I received a revelation about it. From this day, I don't know if I will ever trust these water rituals churches. Typically, trademark of this water churches is marine kingdom association.

Marine kingdom is one of the dangerous satanic mission ever. For the daily lives of the Christian believers are monitored there. They on lookout for the staunch believers to recruit, if not, to destroy. You can even be initiated through dreams and vision. We have to be vigilant and sober.

Chapter 7-Underworld kingdom

One may look at the physical structure of our world with its beauty and assume that's it ends there. Meaning not looking for anything beyond. There is more to life than what we perceive in the physical. In fact, life is more spiritual than physical. We are spirits, soul and body. We resemble the Christian trinity of the Father, son and holy spirit. Beyond the curtains of time there is life and more. I assume prophets, seers and ordinary people who are perceived to be spiritual will agree with me on this one.

The kingdom of darkness has its kingdom in tacked just as the kingdom of God is. The underwater kingdom is where major world meetings are attended. The idea of a new world order is still persisting. The enemy wants to control the whole world with this system. It is totally demonic. The Babylon system of this world is followed by this new world system order whereby the world is ruled by one man.

The marine kingdom is an underwater kingdom structured by the devil to control this world system of politics, finance, education, music etc. The day to day life of every believer or non-believer is monitored in this kingdom. There are position and rank, politicians, religious leaders, musicians, artist or prominent people, majority of them have rank in this kingdom.

Personally, I have seen pastors, celebrities and politicians emerging from waters with power, authority and fame. The church Leader of the Zion Christian Church has a rank in the marine spirit. From a religious standpoint, you look at the trademark of the church. Its products and holy water are the practical stamp of marine kingdom movement. Automatically when you engage in this products you are initiated.

This marine movement is big on dreams and vision. They initiate people through dreams. Whenever you partake on their anointing you reap what they have. This churches have shrines that they pay homage to. For instance, whenever you tithe in church you are growing the alter of marine priest irrespective of how much. by tithing you plant seeds. Just imagine what you will reap seedling to their shrines.

Chapter 8-Mental illnesses

It is widely known in the ZCC that if you do something to the church you are bound to experience problems and misfortune in your life. I was threatened with death and various illnesses, including mental illness if I continued with the book. This book is a spiritual piece of work.

This is not by might or by my power, it is spirit inspired. I was under lot of spiritual attack while on my book mission. Mentally and spiritually, I was ill for a long time. Depressed and stress I was, because of the spiritual abuse and threats I was encountering on the journey. I wasn't surprised because I recalled all the prophecies I used to receive if I ever thought of leaving the church or bad mouthing it in anyhow.

The bishop of the ZCC church will appear in my dreams telling me the dates of my death. We all know he has spiritual powers to do certain things to individual, but my God whom I believe in is the faithful One. He is the shepherd of my soul and preserve of my soul.

Though I was tormented in my mind, I couldn't let that disturb me. It is not in my place to bad mouth any church whatsoever, this is my spiritual journey and a testimony to the body of Christ to be careful with some ministry. We need to be armed and ready spiritually to be victorious in warfare. life is more spiritual than physical. If we can disarm the spiritual oppositions, then we bound to be prosperous in every area.

As a prophet of God, I knew that I was monitored by the marine kingdom. Even my home was bombarded with spiritual cameras and mirror to monitor every way of my move. I have read the bible and various spiritual books, so I knew what I was dealing with. I had to take over the atmosphere and waters by pleading the blood of the lamb to disarm the powers and principalities.

There is this jezebel spirit of mind control that is dealing with majority of believers in the body of Christ. This is what I was dealing with every time. The renewal of mind by the spirit of God is paramount in this case. We are not carnally fighting the war, but spiritually are. For the weapons of our warfare are not carnal, but mighty in the Lord in pulling down the strongholds.

Brethren, we have generational and personal stronghold to defuse. As David fought Goliath, we also have our own Goliath in our lives and our families to neutralize. Knowing the truth, we will be on our way to redemption. Redemption is found in the Lord for he is the foundational truth. Corinthian 10:3 says any thought that highly exalt itself other than the knowledge of God must be held captive and into the obedience of Christ. Christ is the chief cornerstone of every Christian church. We ought to move from the Christian culture to the biblical culture. The idea of being bible based in our doctrine in our African churches. The notion of being picky should automatically end.

Chapter 9-Stubborn ZCC spirits

There is that tendency of no way out. I always ask myself why most of members who left the church their lives a troublesome. To the point whereby some are mental ill while others are experiencing some sort of misfortune in their lives. Broadly member will tell you this church is independent and has all that you need, therefore, you don't just leave it. It will come on you.

There are even circulating prophecies in the church probably by the founders of the church that ZCC you don't just leave it. Basically, He doesn't want any member do go to other churches for prayers and worships. That's why you don't ever see ZCC church mingling with other believers. The body of Christ is built upon the foundation of the apostles and prophets whereas Jesus Christ is the Chief Cornerstone.

Jesus Christ gave to the church prophets, apostles, teachers, evangelist and pastors. These are what we call fivefold ministry-gift to the church. The body of Christ isn't divided. Practically the body of Christ is the body of a person Jesus. Of which the parts on his body work hands in hands, interdependent. I believe churches should also work together as we are under one Christian umbrella. On their part I think maybe it might be numbers because the church has million members.

I personally experience numerous misfortunes trying to leave the church. I wasn't happy with the everyday doctrine I was fed with. I believe spiritual growth is paramount and ideal goal for every member. I will question some doctrine and I will be told that this church is not for those who act like they are wise. I will rather not talk about character and attitudes of some members. This is what we all experience as believers. Brethren love slowly expires every day in churches. We are practically empty vessels who doesn't want to be filled up. Let us rather go back and drink once again from the well of God of Jacob. The fountain of God is love.

OCCULT CHURCH EXPOSED: MY FIRSTHAND TESTIMONY

The prophecies will tell me not to even try to leave the church. I felt threatened of some prophecies. I even had numerous encounters with the leader of the church spiritually telling not to leave the church. There is the promise of misfortune if you ever leave their cult. I believe cult is something that you are not supposed to leave. Danger and destruction are the result thereafter.

I was told I will not get a job or marry if I don't believe in leader of the church. I spend the whole years under spiritual attacks from witches and wizard trying to make my life a living hell. I couldn't even sleep with the amount of spiritual attack I was experiencing. At some point I had to leave my village to the mountain for prayer and fasting.

Glory to the Lord God of heaven who shielded me from all the turmoil. The ship didn't drown because Jesus Christ was in the boat with me. I spend sleepless night in the mountains communing with God about my life. That's where I realize that majority of spirits that we encountering are not all from God. Same as dreams and visions 90% of them are not from God. Biblical dreams and visions should much align with the biblical principles. What we tend to say its an African culture especially of ancestral worship, mixing Christianity with ancestral veneration, while is far from biblical principles of the founding father of all religions, Abraham.

All religions take its roots from the Abrahamic faith apart from the polytheism movement. The idea of one God is paramount in Judaism, Christianity and Islam. Deuteronomy 6:4 "hear, O Israel: The Lord our God, the Lord is one. The monotheism is the notion introduced by God to the founding father of faith Abraham. Abraham hail from the land of Ur where the practices of polytheism was at its highest.

The reason why I am on this oneness of God is that we are slowly adopting other practices derailing us from the biblical truth. I have often noted that while I was in the ZCC we were venerating ancestral spirits. The idea which is against the bible. The prophet will tell you to connect your relative ancestors with the ancestors of the church through Mpogo ritual. Moreover, when you fetching holy water from mountains and rivers you also told to acknowledge the owners of the mountains and rivers. This is more like moving away from the monotheist idea of God.

Chapter 10-Occultism practices

There came the thought to me to leave church denomination to go to others. It did not sit well with the authority. I was bombarded with dreams and visions of the leader of the church angry with me. I was depressed and stressed as my dream life was all about him. At some point I was even told that I joined and there is no way out. That where I realized that I was in the occult movement.

I started astral projecting going to places in the spirit that I don't even know. Sometimes I will hear conversations in my mind. Especially at night while I'm sleeping I would be disturbed by the conversation and the leader of the church will be speaking. God will never forsake or leave his children.

At some point around 7 pm usually I will feel the present of the spirits around the house to accompany me to the rivers. That's where meetings are held, in oceans, lakes and rivers. Witches and wizard hold their meeting in the waters. Psalm 24 {24:1} The earth [is] the LORD'S, and the fullness thereof; the world, and they that dwell therein. {24:2} For he hath founded it upon the seas, and established it upon the floods.

I was given a gold bracelets and chain in the spirit. Usually some receive rings. These material objects are covenants. That means you a part of the cult movement. Honestly speaking, when you are in you are in. there is no turning back unless by the grace and mercy of God. It was not my will to be initiated into the marine kingdom, it was partly because of the church that I was in. it is a marine kingdom church led by the marine cult priest.

You should be caution when you go to waters churches because most of them are under the spirit of marine. The mythical underwater creatures and mermaids powered up the churches. Look at the tables and pulpit of many churches, you will see what I'm talking about. For instance, some put fruits on basket on the table, sort of a decoration. It is basically an alter and that's where the power of the church is.

I spend years crying day and night because I was helplessly having out of body experiences, what I will term astral projection. projection. I wasn't happy because this was the marine kingdom of witchcraft. You can be a witch or wizard unknowingly. Most of our brother and sister suffer the fate of what they don't know. Most of them they are initiated in the marine kingdom but they don't know.

Marine kingdom is the ruthless dark kingdom of witchcraft. Most people are initiated in through dreams. mainly when you start experiencing sexual and eating dreams just know that you are initiated. I was also initiated through dreams similar to those ones. Since majority believe in ancestors, ancestors, the will just shove those serpents dreams and say snakes represents their dead relatives. Snakes are also big in the occult movement. They represent many things across culture.

In the occult practices sex is the big thing. Sex is power. You have to be married to someone or some creature in spirit. It serves as a covenant making in the witchcraft kingdom. To be powerful you have to sleep with someone to awaken your spirituality, but it happens in spirit. As faith is the currency in Christianity, so does sex in the kingdom of the devil. Practices such as musterbation are demonic. Even the watching of pornography. You give these demons access into your life to make your life a living hell. The amount of stagnation brothers and sister are experiencing some maybe be due to these strongholds such as musterbation and pornography. Some people unknowingly initiated themselves in the occult by these practices. I urge you brothers and sisters to stop these detestable acts.

Chapter 11-Prophesy in the church.

Compare Exodus 4:10-16 to 7:1,2 as an example. Moses' was God's mouth because God told him what to say. So Aaron was Moses' mouth or spokesman, because Moses' told him what to say. But Exodus 7:1,2 calls this the work of a "prophet." God → Moses → Aaron → People

Hence, a prophet was a mouthpiece or a spokesman. Prophecy was the ability to speak the will of God by the direct guidance and inspiration of the Holy Spirit. [Vine on "prophecy": "...prophecy is not necessarily, nor even primarily, foretelling. It is the declaration of that which cannot be known by natural means...it is the forth-telling of the will of God, whether with reference to the past, the present, or the future ..."]

[Thayer on "prophet": "...one who, moved by the Spirit of God and hence his organ or spokesman, solemnly declares to men what he has received by inspiration..."]

Prophesy is for edification, exhortation and comfort (Corinthian 14:31). It is a gift to the body of Christ to edify each other in spirit. When the spirit prophesy moves in church, God is at work. It is something else to hear the mind and will of God at our present times. I have noticed that in our mist, ZCC, the spirit of divination governs. The reason being, you have to do something before you can prophesy. Heading to the mountains, fountains and rivers for spiritual awakening is part and parcel of the call.

When Christ ascended he gave men gifts, some to be prophets, apostles, evangelist, preachers and teachers. It is a gift to the body of Christ. Same applies, at the day of Pentecost, the apostle received the gift of the holy spirit. Meaning we are in the receiving mode. Christ is the giver. He doesn't require any assistance. All we have to do is tarry and wait for manifestation. There is really no need to do certain things to receive gifts from God.

The mercy and grace of God is sufficient enough. God is enough by himself. We can worship, pray and fast but it's by his will. Practically as Christians we are all urged to fast and pray at some point in our lives. But fasting doesn't move God, it moves us towards the mind and will of God.

What I noted from our brothers and sister is the idea of trying to meet God halfway. Almighty God doesn't need our help; he needs our heart. The language of God is a heart to heart talk. Meaning God is spirit. His spirits Is within our heart and abide with us. The anointing of God is internal and external. It is within us and also upon us to perform wonders. He is really a wonder and miracle working God.

In the ZCC you will have someone coming from the lineage of Sangoma initiated to be prophets. You can go to perform ancestral rituals of initiation (Go Thwasa) and come back to prophesy in the church. The spirit of divination is taking over. And it is the dangerous spirit because it hails from the marine kingdom.

The sad truth is that some of our ancestors used to bow down to these mythical creatures such as merman and mermaid. Some bowing down to animals, trees, waters and mountain creatures, these spirits are generational. They will work around the family line from time to time. These are not clean spirits because they affect your body in a worse way. You hardly see a good looking individual who undergo the initiation process of working a prophet of this type.

It is only a handful believers who are led by the holy spirit. We are baptized in the name of the Father, Son, and Holy Spirit - Matthew 28:19. The holy spirit is the third person of the trinity. "Trinity" is a word for three persons in the one Godhead. The caution is that not all spirits are from God. Not all dreams and visions are from God. The spirit of discernment is there to help us discern which spirit is active and in operation. Mainly it helps us to divide the truth from deceptions. The supernatural ability to distinguish true prophets or teachings from false (1 Corinthians 12:10; cf. 1 John 4:1). John 14:16,17,26; (15:26; 16:7,13)

Jesus promised to send to the apostles "the Comforter" even "the Spirit of Truth." But in 14:26 He calls the one He would send the "Holy Spirit." So, "Spirit of Truth" and "Comforter" here are simply other names for the Holy Spirit. Witchcraft prophecies would not comfort the believers. Usually this types prophecies such as prophesying that your family is against you or your in-law cursed you will bareness or joblessness, they come from other spirits other than the holy spirit. The holy spirit act in accordance with the word of God. The spirit of divination bring fear over faith. We are the faith based believers.

Chapter 12-The position of the bishop

When discussing the Christology of the ZCC, another important question is: what position does bishop Lekganyane hold in the beliefs of ZCC-members and how does this influence the Christology of the church? One way of investigating the position of bishop Lekganyane in the ZCC, is to read the praise poems that appear regularly in The ZCC Messenger. These poems contain a wealth of titles bestowed on the bishop, and some amazing pronouncements about him. Furthermore, many articles sing the praises of the ZCC and, especially, of its leader.

Occasionally the bishop allows insight into how he sees himself when he speaks about himself, his father and his grandfather. We shall firstly take a look at the different titles given to the bishop and secondly, analyse some statements made about him, either by others or himself.

Ramarumo

The title most often used for Lekganyane is Ramarumo, which means: father of the spears. Obviously this title conveys the message that Lekganyane is very powerful. An example from a praise poem is the following:

Ntate Ramarumo,

ruri o tlo buia dikgutlo tsa lefase kaofela,

which means:

Father, Ramarumo, he will really rule all the comers of the earth.

Kgomo

The name Kgomo that is used in this poem, is found in many other praise poems and articles as well. Apparently the kgomo (head of cattle) is the totem animal of the Lekganyane family At the same time, considering the tremendous importance of cattle for the African people traditionally, it is understandable that this name gains 'surplus value'. The name acquires additional imagery by suggesting that Lekganyane: is the one to feed and sustain the people.

Kganya

The name Kganya means: Light It is another name used for Lekganyane. An example "Lord Lekganyane you are the guardian of all people. Your glory is on the whole world. Your love is amazing, in heaven, and everywhere on earth. We say, Kganya, ask wisdom or us in heaven."

Mookamedi

The most common title for Lekganyane is Mookamedi, which corresponds to the Greek episkopos (one who watches over, an overseer, guardian). The word is derived from the verb go okamela, which means: look down, watch over, supervise. A mookamedi is thus a supervisor, a guardian, someone who watches over. Zionists, when speaking about Lekganyane, would often not use his surname but rather refer to 'the Mookamedi'. The title 'Mookamedi' in itself does not give Lekganyane divine or messianic status. Initially it probably was nothing more than a translation of the English word 'bishop'.

Mediator

Another title frequently applied to Lekganyane is 'Mediator'. The last quotation from PM Kubayi illustrated this, with the words: "No Zionists can ask something from God, or communicate with God, except through you!" That this sort of statement is no incident, can be proved by many other examples. A short list reads as follows: PM Kubayi, in another article under the telling title 'The Right Reverend Bishop B.E. Lekganyane is the present day Mediator between the Zionists and gods and God', writes as follows;

"I publicly proclaim that (the Right Reverend Bishop of the mighty Zion Christian Church) is the Mediator between the people and God. He is the way to God. No one can communicate with God except through Him. He is the only person who reveals God's will to the human beings. He is the only person who can communicate with our gods. Through His message, the prophets and the ministers of Zion Christian Church, God's will is proclaimed to the people. My fellow Zionists, you are fortunate, because you have the Mediator or Spokesman. I am saying this from experience. experience. At this moment I have experienced the power of Zion Christian Church through our Mediator. My fellow Zionists, as a teacher, I have realised that in our Mediator, all things are possible, especially if you respect and obey "ditaelo" from God through our Mediator".

How the member sees him?

I would be lying if I say the members of the church doesn't see him as God. The spirit of the church testifies what I am saying. The prophet prophecy in his name. they will tell you thus speak the God of the church Barnabas Lekganyane. The three patriarchal leaders are at the center stage in the lives of the ZCC members. These are some of the names he bears:

✓ Kgomo (Cow)
✓ Sebata se se golo (Big creature)
✓ Holy spirit
✓ Mediator between God and ancestors
✓ Messiah
✓ Jesus Christ
✓ Leswika (Rock of ages)
✓ Modimo wa thaba Sione (God of Mount Zion)
✓ "Kgosi ya dikgosi" (King of kings)
✓ "Lion of Judah, descendant of the House of David"
✓ "our Father, our Healer, our Comforter"
✓ "beloved Son of man",
✓ "Son of God"
✓ "the messenger of God"
✓ "light of the nations, head of everything"
✓ "Rrago ditshaba" (Father of the nations)
✓ "moya o mokgethwa" (the holy spirit)
✓ "moleti wa bohle" (guardian of all)
✓ "tselayago yago Modimo Ntate" (the way to go to God the Father)

These are but some of the few names he bears as a leader of the church. Although according to Zion Cristian members. Majority of members lack sound doctrine. I once had a priest on the podium saying that as the Zion member even if you don't read the bible is okay because God blessed them with prophets. Initially it is the call of all the prophet to direct people to sound biblical doctrine. To rebuke, correct and direct believers in the ways of the Lord. This can only be achieved through bible. A prophet without the word of God is like a fish without water.

Chapter 13-Spiritual prisons

I don't know if you are familiar with the concept of prisons in the marine, underworld and second heaven. But they are there. The enemy has also perverted ways of the Lord. He resembled all the kingdoms of God in his kingdom. Sadly, we think Satan rule in the hades. The enemy has a kingdom up there in the second heaven (Between the third heaven and the earth). Our very own sky that we see with our naked eyes is the first heaven. God didn't create heaven but heavens!

When you bind the demon it is bound in the spiritual prisons. A human soul can also be captured. Especially those who are in the works of the witchcraft they know very well that soul can be bound. My soul was in prison in the Lekganyane kingdom for a long time. Because in this type of churches, they are no way out. It is by the grace of God I was victorious at the end. People this church is in the kingdom of darkness! There's no salvation of souls in the ZCC.

There is no where were you accept the Lord Jesus Christ as your saviour. The is only baptism of water which is linked to the marine powers. They will just say we baptize you in the name of the Father, Son and Holy spirit but they know who resembles the Father, Son and Holy spirit. If they were worshipping the same God we worship they would not rebuke me for using the name of Jesus. Anyone who doesn't have the Son, doesn't have the Father.

I will always sense the bad spirits around me. Especially in my room, I could sense that something is not adding up. With God grace my eyes were open in the spirit and I could see demons. I was accompanied by human souls that were recording whatever I was doing daily.

These are what you will call the marine spirits spiritual camera. They are planted in homes to see what people are doing daily. You will think some of the priest are real prophets while they planted things in homestead of the believers. The body of Christ need to wake up and be vigilant at all times. We are already in a war whether you like it or not. But my God is bigger than any other foreign god.

The blood of Jesus is weapon of destruction upon the camp of the enemy. I will hear the voice of the demons in my ears convincing me that Lekganyane is God. There is no other God besides him. These are what I will hear daily.

The threats, false hope and hopeless prophecies of amounting to nothing. The Lord of mercy and grace will never leave or forsake you people. Believe in God alone you will experience his power. For his grace is sufficient. Let us be like Paul who fought the good fight of faith. Rest assured, victory is ours!

Chapter 14-Initiation into witchcraft

I will always thank the Almighty God for blessing me with the spiritual senses. Recently the church is slowly losing its grip of the discerning of the spirits. Discernment of spirit is the underrated gift yet powerful. Because the idea of good and evil is here for long haul. While I was a ZCC member I used to have encounters with Barnabas Lekganyane in dreams and vision laying hands on me.

I thought I was the chosen once since it's a tradition in the church that if he appears to you in dreams, you are blessed and highly favoured. I thought so, unbeknown to me that he was initiating me into the kingdom of witchcraft (Marine kingdom). I will helplessly watch my soul coming out of my body. Having out of body experiences, seeing different places, people etc. I didn't know what was happening to me.

Later I knew that I was in the darkness. In the church of ZCC we were too fascinated about the idea of river and mountain creatures. You can't spend the whole month without heading to the streams and mountains. I came across the idea of marine spirit when I had an encounter with the Lord Jesus Christ. I started dealing with the marine spirit, renouncing and denouncing them. Though it not a child plays to cut the ties with the waters. It is by God grace to be victorious in this area.

You cannot serve God and ancestors at the same time. They are more like two masters. The ways of the Lord and ancestors are different. The Lord ways are always perfect. The ancestors were not so perfect. Even the revered names of the biblical patriarchal were not so. The Lord ways are perfect and righteous. Only Jesus Christ resembles the likeness of the Father. He is the perfect example to us as the body of Christ. He is the hope and glory to the body of Christ.

Apostle Paul throughout the book of Ephesians introduces warfare to us. We aren't fighting humans but spiritual entities of wickedness that governs the atmosphere. Every country, city and village has its principalities and powers that governs the atmosphere. In my village the spirit of witchcraft is so strong. These tells you the spirit that is ruling in the village. For instance, if the region where you from crime is a big thing. Then the spirit of crime is in the territory. Life is spiritual. Most of manipulations happens in the spirit. Destinies are stolen and manipulated in the spirit.

As Christians already we are in the warfare. Whether you like it or not, at some point you have to fight. Apostle Paul had also thorns in the flesh. We have our own Goliath and Delilahs to fight. Moses went head to head with Pharaoh. Jesus Christ was on the run from King Herod. The nation of Israel throughout history they had philistines and medianites as their enemies. The initiation of witchcraft happens in the second heaven. That's why witches and wizards fly at night in the atmosphere. The second heaven link they stronghold through this sky.

There are thrones and powers in the sky. I have had numerous encounters with spirit of wickedness in the sky. We as Christian we have authority over every power of the enemy. We have the power to bind and loose. Above all, the precious blood of Jesus Christ. We are already victorious we just have to claim our victory. Stay strong and steadfast! Because we have to fight the good fight of faith.

Occultic Practices (Sex is power)

I always thought that the Bishop of the ZCC was a man of God. We all know how members of the church how much revere his name. it is actually surprising how they acknowledge him in all things. During may stay in the church every little thing member attain in life, it is all due to the grace of their Bishop. Especially things like newly born babies, jobs, promotions and marriages.

He is highly revered than the name of God or rather the name of Jesus. He is depicted as the most holy man. But what surprising is that they will say he is able to meditate between their ancestors. ancestors. While we all know that God the Almighty is against someone who venerate or commune with the spirit of the dead. I highly regard the church of Zion as polytheism. There was a time where I will fast. Coz we all know that fasting equips one spiritually. Suddenly, the bishop will come spiritually to sleep with me. I didn't know that sex was that powerful to the point where you can steal some power from someone. It continued for a long time to the point where I even felt hopeless.

Now I realize that in a certain kingdom sex is used as a powerful weapon. Especially in the act of witchcraft sex is powerful. Things like spiritual wife and spiritual husband conjured up so the they can weaken the spirit of men and women. Majority of men and women of God in the body of Christ are suffering because of these stubborn spirit of perversion.

This may be new to the ears of the Zionist who love him so much. But fact remains, the man of God is in deep occultic business. In the business whereby the is no way out. Occultism requires sacrifices from time to time. Some of the member unknowingly are the victim of this occult.

Chapter 15 Is the God of Engenas, Edward and Barnabas the God of the bible?

I have come to the conclusion that the God of Israel is not the same God of Engenas. Without a doubt I can attest that ZCC has moved away from the biblical principle and culture but has adopted the traditions of men. Most of religion subscribe to the 10 commandment of Moses but the polytheism movement has disqualified ZCC from the Abrahamic faith.

The idea of One God may be preached but not practiced. They adhere to some laws; they choose whichever fit. I don't know any Christian church that venerate ancestral worship than ZCC. Ancestral worship is prohibited in the Bible.

Isaiah {8:19} And when they shall say unto you, seek unto them that have familiar spirits, and unto wizards that peep, and that mutter: should not a people seek unto their God? for the living to the dead? {8:20} To the law and to the testimony: if they speak not according to this word, [it is] because [there is] no light in them.

Prophet Isaiah is against those who invoke the spirit of the dead. There is a reason why we say rest in peace when someone has passed away. We believe and rest assured the have fallen and went to the other side. Why bother the dead? Isn't that they should be at peace?

Ecclesiastes {9:5} For the living know that they shall die: but the dead know not anything, neither have they any more a reward; for the memory of them is forgotten.

The enemy has shifted our eyes to what matters the most. God is the jealous God who doesn't want his children to show any affection to other gods. Ancestral worship is another pagan religion which is in conflict with the God of the bible. This is the reason why God said you should have no other Gods before me. Exodus 20 is the foundation of all Abrahamic religion, Judaism, Christianity and Islam. The God of Abraham,

Isaac and Jacob is the monotheist God. Omnipotent God. Supreme God who is the God of all nations.

There is so much paganism practices in ZCC to the point where they even worship images of the bishop. It is actually a command and tradition of the church to have images of the bishop adorning houses of the members. The prophet within a church will tell you to pray unto these pictures because they can see and hear everything. The ZCC has forgotten the Father who art in the heaven. It is actually my plea to go back to the prayers Jesus taught his disciples.

Isaiah {2:22} Cease ye from man, whose breath [is] in his nostrils: for wherein is he to be accounted of?

Stop honouring men more than God. Man of God should the congregation to God not to himself. The idea of man God in Africa must see an end. African brother and sisters respect men of God more than God himself. We want to be taught bible while we idling. Bible can be used as a weapon of power to oppress, and can also be used to transform. People lets be bible based believers who can rightly divide the scriptures. In the ZCC church is all about obeying what the bishop is saying, not what the bible is saying. This is a spiritual dictatorship whereby millions of members are unfamiliar with the name of Jesus Christ but the name Barnabas.

There is only one name under the sun for which believers subscribe to. And that is the name of Jesus Christ. You cannot name the church Zion Christian Church and not be under the head of all churches, Jesus Christ. It is high time we question the foundation of the ZCC.

Ephesians 2:20 And are built upon the foundation of the apostles and prophets, Jesus Christ himself being the chief corner [stone;] {2:21} In whom all the building fitly framed together groweth unto an holy temple in the Lord: {2:22} In whom ye also are builded together for an habitation of God through the Spirit.

The central point of any Christianity is to be like Christ. Christ is the perfect example within the cloud of witness in all religious body. Apostle Paul says follow me as I follow Christ, it means Christ is the final destination. The destination of every member of Zion Christian Church should be Jesus Christ in action and deeds. We pray to God Almighty in the name of Jesus Christ, not in any other name. I direct this message to our brothers and sisters.

Chapter 16-Manipulation of dreams

The Apostle Peter said, "We are His witnesses!" (Acts 5:32) Charity explains how even in receiving prophetic dreams we become 'witnesses' and 'observers' as one of the mechanisms through which God transforms our hearts and minds. Our practiced 'observation' of these 'visions in the night' become revelatory portals through which we pull heaven to earth. Her explanation of this process is revolutionary.

The Bible has much to say about dreams and visions, and it's important to understand that they have great power to change your life. Dreams are absolutely the will of God. They always have been—and so much the more now for us who live in the last of the last days. Joel's prophecy is pointing to you and me.

Dreams are important to God as they are to us. We see in the old testament bible that God communicate through dreams. It is still evident even today. Though there are different voices. One from the enemy. One from God. You have to be spiritually filled to even discern the manner of dreams.

John {4:1} Beloved, believe not every spirit, but try the spirits whether they are of God: because many false prophets are gone out into the world. {4:2} Hereby know ye the Spirit of God: Every spirit that confesseth that Jesus Christ is come in the flesh is of God: {4:3} And every spirit that confesseth not that Jesus Christ is come in the flesh is not of God: and this is that [spirit] of antichrist, whereof ye have heard that it should come; and even now already is it in the world.

This scripture clearly indicate that we need to be spirit filled believer to test every spirit of prophecy, dreams and vision. The reason why I talk about dreams is because the leader of the church moves much in these area. He manoeuvres through dreams in the life of his member. ZCC member will attest to this one. Dreams are respected in ZCC as they believe is the instrument link the living and the dead use to communicate. The man of God shun publicity however in dream he appears to many. It is widely known in the church that to see him in dream is a blessing. Unbeknown that he initiates them into occultism! I am the victim of this.

The marine kingdom is big on dreams and vision, but it is all manipulation, deception and lies. He will initiate you through dreams into witchcraft and implies that the ancestors want you to continue with their work. I have seen the underworld, marine kingdom and second heaven where they initiate member into little witches and wizard!

I used to have a big snake coming to take me into the ocean at night. But I will see it in the spirit though. I would spend countless time fasting and praying to God for this thing. If I hate the ZCC church it would be for a good reason. But we are not to be agent of hate but love.

This book is to warn masses about occultism and witchcraft taking place in ZCC. To expose the amount of spiritual abuse I have endured for so long. It is time up the church take it stance on what is right. It is so saddening how the man of God is wholly revered by millions. He is not what many think he is. The Babylon system must see its way out in the church of Jesus Christ. It is all about Christ. Not about the agenda of someone's family.

Jude {1:4} For there are certain men crept in unawares, who were before of old ordained to this condemnation, ungodly men, turning the grace of our God into lasciviousness, and denying the only Lord God, and our Lord Jesus Christ.

I have stated earlier in other chapters than the leader Barnabas prays to Indian deities. The one revealed to me is Lord Shiva and other Canaan ancient god such as Moloch, who is known for child sacrifice. The Lord Jesus Christ is preached and worshipped by member but he is absent. It is hard to believe I know, but is not just an ordinary, it is a revelation I received from God. It is not by might, or by power, but it is by the spirit of the living God. The amount of spiritual abuse and threats I enduring during the writing of this book was unbearable.

Chapter 17-Misinterpretation of scriptures

It is a common thing in the body of Christ to misinterpret scriptures. Even the pillars of the churches of the likes of Apostle Peter was finding it hard to understand some of Paul's writing. The word of God requires the renewal of mind and spirit. The eyes and mind of understanding must be open to grasp the word.

The word is the sword of the spirit. We need the holy spirit in order to articulate the mind and will of God. I have observed that the misinterpretation of scripture in ZCC is big. Not only in ZCC, but matter of fact, the whole body of The word is the sword of the spirit. We need the holy spirit in order to articulate the mind and will of God. I have observed that the misinterpretation of scripture in ZCC is big. Not only in ZCC, but matter of fact, the whole body Christ lacks the basis of right theology. The traditions of men are at the forefront of churches.

A Rammutla writes (translated from Northern Sotho): He who puts his trust in our helper B.E. Lekganyane, will have peace in the midst of many difficulties. Because our mookamedi knows what we need. Put off the old man and put on the new man and let us follow our mookamedi. Because he is the way to go to God the Father.

" PM Kubayi writes

"Besides what I have stated above, there are still some more examples which can be given to prove that the Right Reverend Bishop B.E. Lekganyane is the present-day Messiah. First of all, it is a well-known fact that Jesus was a religious Messiah, and not a political Messiah. I think I shall be quite right to state that our present-day mediator is not a political mediator. He is the peace-maker. He is a king of peace. As a result, He expects his followers to be peace-makers at all times. Secondly, Jesus used to heal the sick when he was on earth. This function is fulfilled by our mediator. He also heals the sick. Thirdly, Jesus used to travel from one place to another, spreading the Word of God, and also doing miracles. Our mediator also travels from one country to another, e.g. he has already visited the countries such as ga-Muila, ga-Mulima, Nzhelele, Giyani, Bochem, Transkei, Kimberley, Secunda, Tafelkop, QwaQwa, New York, London, Washington D.C. etc. At each of these places, miracles miracles occurred, e.g. at ga-Muila and other places, rain fell, although they had no rain in the past. At ga-Mulima the farmers got much harvest, but this was not the case prior to His visit. At QwaQwa, people had no rain for a couple of months, but when our Bishop visited visited there on the 9th -11 December 1989, it rained cats and dogs."

The same PM Kubayi writes in another article To the Right Reverend Bishop BE Lekganyane, I say, "Kgomo", I have experienced that you are indeed the true Messiah and the true Mediator between the Zionists and God. No Zionist can ask something from God, or communicate with God, except through you!" These are articles from Zion Christian Church publication called Messenger. These writers with no equivocal, believes that the Right Reverend Bishop Lekganyane is Jesus Christ. While some writings claim that he is the holy spirit. We have one mediator between man and God, the man Jesus Christ. Clearly Bishop Lekganyane isn't the one who hang on the cross in Jerusalem for the redemption of mankind. This is the plain truth. Now we are in the times of the holy spirit, the times prophesied by the prophet Joel.

Joel {2:28} And it shall come to pass afterward, [that] I will pour out my spirit upon all flesh; and your sons and your daughters shall prophesy, your old men shall dream dreams, your young men shall see visions: {2:29} And also upon the servants and upon the handmaids in those days will I pour out my spirit.

This prophecy was fulfilled in the time of the apostle in the day of Pentecost. The spirit of the Lord came upon them. Not that a person came embodied the spirit himself, but the spirit of the Lord came upon them all.

Act {2:1} And when the day of Pentecost was fully come, they were all with one accord in one place. {2:2} And suddenly there came a sound from heaven as of a rushing mighty wind, and it filled all the house where they were sitting. {2:3} And there appeared unto them cloven tongues like as of fire, and it sat upon each of them. {2:4} And they were all filled with the Holy Ghost, and began to speak with other tongues, as the Spirit gave them utterance.

Sadly, the member of the church venerates Lekganyane as God. We can see the claims above. And in the you are not prohibited to pray in the name of Lekganyane. In fact, it is emphasized that you should connect your ancestor with the Lekganyane ancestors for blessings. Many members can attest. I believe the fact that he appears in their dreams might be the reason for these claims. I have been a member I know what I am talking about. My life changed dramatically when I had an encounter with Jesus Christ. And the most misquoted scriptures are Psalm 2:6, 110 and Micah 4:5.

Psalm {2:6} Yet have I set my king upon my holy hill of Zion.

This is the most quoted scripture in the ZCC churches. The Psalmist, David, was taking about himself here as chosen vessel by God to be the king of all Israel ruling in the holy hills of Zion, in Jerusalem. Because all the other heathen Kings were against him and his kingdom. The psalm also foreshadows Jesus Christ who will sit upon the throne of his ancestor, David. The house of David is chosen by God as his scepter: power and authority of God. The tribe of Judah is chosen by God to be the spiritual leader in all ages, thus Jesus and king David fulfilled this scripture. This psalm is messianic.

Psalm {110:4} The LORD hath sworn, and will not repent, Thou [art] a priest for ever after the order of Melchizedek.

This scripture talks about someone who is a priest forever. Who is the priest forever? Jesus Christ is. He fulfilled this prophecy when he went to the cross as the lamb of God. Apostle Paul went deeper on this one on Hebrews chapter 7. Christ still mediate and plead to God for us. Clearly someone who dies wouldn't fit this scripture.

Micah {4:1} But in the last days it shall come to pass, [that] the mountain of the house of the LORD shall be established in the top of the moun-

tains, and it shall be exalted above the hills; and people shall flow unto it. {4:2} And many nations shall come, and say, Come, and let us go up to the mountain of the LORD, and to the house of the God of Jacob; and he will teach us of his ways, and we will walk in his paths: for the law shall go forth of Zion, and the word of the LORD from Jerusalem.

Let us go to the house of God of Jacob. Is ZCC serving the God of Jacob? The same God of Abraham, Isaac and Jacob? The God of the ancient prophet? The Torah? The laws of God never change. Malachi {3:6} For I [am] the LORD, I change not; therefore, ye sons of Jacob are not consumed. Again, is ZCC bible based in their theocracy? This scripture point to us to Israel. The messiah came from the line of Judah. The nations will also look unto Judah for the teachings of God. Jesus Christ is a Jew. He also died as a Jew. He is the chief cornerstone of the church. The foundation of Christianity is the Jewish messiah. All shall look unto the nation of Israel. Judah is still the scepter of God.

Chapter 18-Honouring material objects than God

It pretty a shame that these days we are trying so hard to put God in the background. It is all about honoring materials as holier than the one who makes them holy. We are the generation of oils, holy water, various cosmetics and branded product in the church of Jesus Christ. People with branded holy items but with weak Christology. We are too materialistic in the house of God. In the times of Moses, God only allowed table, lamp and holy vessel. Nowadays church turned out to be businesses. Making millions selling branded product termed "holy".

The traditions of men make the Word of God of no effect. Any tradition, religious or otherwise, that keeps us from experiencing and knowing the living Christ (Truth) is a tradition that needs to be discarded. Our tradition has blinded our eyes of understanding to see the truth. Truth is what shall set most of us true. Because we are believing the white lie and we don't know it. The practises of men brings bondages. It doesn't matter some things have been practised for centuries, but if it doesn't instil peace, it need to be questioned. churches have their own rules and cultures. Some of them are just man made rule with no biblical doctrines.

It is all about coming with ideas that will make the church money. Member of the church honors their church attires as holier. I wonder if they give the same respect to God as how much they honor their church clothes and products such as salt, and branded tea. Mountains and rivers are more respected.

The occultism operates in the spirit of fear. Anything that opposes the spirit of the Lord is of the enemy. The enemy does not operate in faith but fear. He will instil fear in you so that you can always fear him. The Lord is love. Everything that comes from God is out of Love. Even the Judgments that befall Sodom and Gomorrah it was out of love. But with our understanding we will look at God as being unjust. God is slow to anger, full of mercy and love. He certainly gave the more than enough time to repent.

The spirit of fear is what is gripping many Christians in the body of Christ. The enemy is working overtime to destroy believers. He hates us with a passion. If you are not doing any impact in the kingdom of darkness, he will not play along. I have noticed the spirit of fear in ZCC through prophecy. The prophets will bombard you with how they want to bewitch you, how your family are against you and how your neighbours and community are jealous of you. They will instil fear in you to always run to their churches whenever see fit. This is a way of luring and controlling the congregation through spirit of fear.

* * * *

THE SPIRIT OF PROPHECY is for edifying the church. It is certainly not for condemnation. We are not in bondage but in freedom through Christ. That's why we should always walk in the light. It is actually mesmerising how they are all afraid of their bishop. He is termed as holy and dangerous man. Some will say you are playing with fire when you speaking about him.

To their very own intellectual he has the God status quo. Even the priests on the pulpit will teach about him not Christ about how powerful he is. The idea here is to fear man not God. I wish it was the other way round. For the word of God say blessed is he who trust in the Lord. Cursed is he who trust in men.

A covenant is often compared to a contract, but biblical covenant goes much deeper. Generally, a contract is limited to the legal obligations between parties. Covenant touches moral and spiritual obligations. Covenant is when you make an agreement. It may be a physical or spiritual, it does not matter. Soul ties are spiritual covenant. Majority of believers they know what soul ties are and how much they can have an impact in their lives.

Most of the time we dwell on the negative side of soul ties but there a some positive one. David sword was knit with Nathaniel sword. This was a healthy and friendly friendship. When partners get married, they become one. You become one with what you marry into. I am saying all of these because I struggled a lot with ungodly ties.

Someone in the kingdom of witchcraft can marry you in the spirit. Then you will always be with him or her together in spirit in the kingdom of darkness. Two is better than one. Because you empower each other spiritually. Even deeper, you can engage in a spiritual sex. Most of the people who struggle with spiritual husband and wife, these are some of the case.

I have spent almost 10 years struggling with women sleeping with me in dreams. The ZCC church don't have much revelation about the marine kingdom. I have said in other chapters; it is on the marine kingdom movement. The covenant is affecting many church members. You will find men and women of God in valleys and streams of rivers performing what they can "Ditaelo" trying to dispel spiritual entities that appear sexually in their dreams. They want only your blood. It is all about the blood in the kingdom of darkness. Much like Christianity as it is about the death of Jesus Christ.

The sad thing is that these spirits comes from the water. The mermaids and mermen, that claim many believers as their partners. These are some of the fallen creatures' people worship throughout our African cultures. Most prophecies in ZCC will send people to mountains and rivers for worship, cleansing and purification. I have often discovered that in these places, you encounter the gods and goddess, there is no God. You form ties with these gods of the mountains and goddess of the rivers. These are some of the dangerous spirit to commune with. Spirit filled believers should only seek the Lord, not bow down to these detestable practices.

Blood strengthen the power of both kingdoms. The kingdom of God and kingdom of Satan. The enemy will always try to pervert the things of God. many well-known rich people are paying a huge price by sacrificing their lives to Devil in exchange of power, fame and money.

The enemy didn't want the release of this book. Thus I suffered tremendously spiritually. I used to hear the voice of the Zion Christian Church Leader, Barnabas Lekganyane everyday threatening to kill me if I release a book. At night I can also feel my spirit Astra project. That's what they do in the occultic business. You are no longer in control of your soul. Your soul is in the position of another man.

It is strange however he calls himself the man of God. while he is in the business of initiating member into the occultism. Bear in mind that I never joined the occultic, I joined the church. Unbeknown to me that it is full of occultism. We all know that witchcraft is creeping speedily in the body of Christ.

You wonder why African churches are full of witchcraft, occult and Satanism. It is because of such leader of calibre who will go all out to experiment with foreign powers. They will go to different religion and make something out of all religion. We have Christian who are experimenting with African traditional ritual of healing and power. Countries such as Nigeria and Ghana are hot spot for these Bishops, pastors and prophet to acquire power to wow their followers with miracles and healing. Indian healing and rituals have been practised in Christianity for long haul. The mind control power is big in this business. As you want to be able to control your followers. Specially to do what you say. Satan wants to control the minds of all the inhabitants of the world in order to force them to worship him. God, on the other hand, gives us liberty to love and serve Him. All the mind controlling I went through, were all a way for him to be worshipped as God. As we pointed out in Ezekiel 13:18-21, Witchcraft steals the souls of men and women. The soul contains the intellect, emotions, and will.

I had a revelation whereby my eyes opened and saw all the souls that work for Lekganyane. I also grew around a village where witchcraft is at its heights. Someone will be buried today but you will see him at night.

Let's pray for Africa. Witchcraft is real. A person who is under the power of the Witchcraft Mind Control spirit finds himself subject to uncontrollable urges and thoughts. Certain emotions and feelings arise unexpectedly. Despondency and mood swings mark his personality. He feels compelled to do certain things or to act in certain ways. Often, anger and bitterness emerge unexpectedly and just as quickly subside.

S atan's most powerful weapon is deception. Second Thessalonians 2:3 says, "Let no man deceive you by any means: for that day shall not come, except there comes a falling away first, and that man of sin be revealed, the son of perdition." In the end times, many saints will fall away from the faith because of deception. Jesus Himself warns of deception (Matt. 24:12, 24). Revelation 13:14 says that Satan 's beast will deceive the whole world (except the mature in God) into worshipping him.

Deceived people do not know that they are deceived. They have accepted lies as truth. They absolutely believe the lies that the enemy has fed them. Their minds are set and controlled by Satan, the father of lies (John 8:44). Mind is an important intellectual property to God. The enemy is after the mind of believers more than anything. Deception is a way of luring Christians to succumb to the devil. The plan of the enemy is to kill, steal and destroy the believers. That why Jesus Christ has to come, but to destroy the works of the darkness.

The word soul refers to the mind, emotions, and will. A soul tie is the binding of our mind and emotions to something that can influence our behaviour. A soul tie can also affect our will and the choices we make. The Bible makes references to good and bad soul ties. In Genesis 2:24, God describes His plan for a godly soul tie relationship—it is called marriage. God spoke His plan for marriage into existence in the Garden of Eden: *For this reason, a man will leave his father and mother and be united to his wife, and they will become one flesh* (Genesis 2:24).

His Word is very specific about how we are to conduct ourselves in sexual relationships. The sex act is permitted only between a man and the woman to whom he is married. The institution of marriage was created by God, in part as a divine plan for procreation. It permits the joining of flesh between a man and a woman; it also allows the continuation of the human race.

Yet, Ephesians 5 reveals a higher meaning and purpose to God's one-flesh plan of marriage. The union of marriage is the earthly model of our heavenly union with Christ: "For this reason a man will leave his father and mother and be united to his wife, and the two will become one flesh." *This is a profound mystery—but I am talking about Christ and the church* (Ephesians 5:31-32).

Voices in my head

The moment I started thinking of releasing the book, I started experiencing spiritual blockage and mental irregular. I battled with demonic voices for some time now. I will have sleepless night being condemned and threatened by the church leaders. He will make threats and accusations. Why I left the church, He is God, this and that.

We all know our Father who art in heaven right? I will lose concentration of what matters most in life listening to evil voices. Though sometimes I will be afraid at times. The road wasn't easy at all. But through God there is always a way. a Light at the end of the tunnel indeed. He will always manipulate, lie and deceive me with his voices. It would be like I am having a conversation with someone in my mind. What they usually call telepathy-mind to mind talk. It is also controlling. My mind will wander speaking to these spirits day and night. I even decided to takes medication because I was always anxious and tired.

At night I will feel like someone is projecting his thoughts in my mind and I will respond unconsciously. The spirit of mind control is real guys. You wonder why people do strange things involuntarily. involuntarily. This is a stronghold I struggled with for very long time. Especially during the drafting of these book. All hell broke loose on me. But it was supposed to be like that since this is a revelatory book. I am revealing what the spirit of the Lord told me. The biblical verse that kept me going is 2 Corinthian 10:3 {10:4} (For the weapons of our warfare [are] not carnal, but mighty through God to the pulling down of strong holds;) {10:5} Casting down imaginations, and every high thing that exalteth itself itself against the knowledge of God, and bringing into captivity every thought to the obedience of Christ.

Marine Kingdom

The power of the Marine Kingdom is the center for the Principalities, Powers, Ruling Spirits and wicked spirits who will possess the world rulers in the end time. "For we wrestle not against flesh and blood, but against principalities, against powers, against the rulers of the darkness of this world, against spiritual wickedness in high places," (Eph. 6:12).

This is the supreme dangerous kingdom so far within the body of Satanism. Many lives are captured under the seas and monitored by the devil himself. As the body of Christ we shouldn't sleep on this kingdom because we are mostly affected and enslaved. Satan agenda is to keep us ignorant of his devices. The Marine Kingdom is the highest influential power of the fallen evil forces of all demonic kingdoms on the earth. Satan's hosts dwelling in the sea are known as marine spirits. The Marine demonic empire is extremely wicked well organized monarchy on earth. The dominate center of operations is located within the India Sea.

These water demons rule over government; work in marriages and divorces that take place worldwide. All sexual activities are being manipulated by marine kingdom evil forces. The Marine Kingdom are given assignments and also responsible for the following problems affecting many mankind: accidents; shortage of blood in one's body; bankruptcy; sudden loss of business; sudden death; chronic spinsterhood; bachelorhood; sudden loss of pregnancy (miscarriages); barrenness; regular eating and eating disorders; drinking; dreams; constant swimming in the dream; demonic spiritual husband/wife; and children problems. Also, Marine human agents' problems (those they possessed) without the people knowing.

Sleeping with creatures at night

People out there are really suffering and being tormented by evil spirits. encountering demonic powers having night visitations by spirits that are sexually attacking them; many mentally ill, crippled blinded, sick and emotionally tormented. Sadly, majority of us lack a thorough knowledge in demonology. Christian and non-believer alike, would go to psychiatrist and psychologies to matters concerning spirits. Spiritual matters for spiritual solutions.

Satan has a demonic kingdom and ignoring it will not make the tormenting spirits stop their work. Matter of fact, Satan's witchcraft world works by remaining secret and once he has captured a person, their only hope for deliverance by the powerful name of Jesus Christ. People parish because of lack of knowledge. I had to do research and thorough study about this subject because I was once a victim. I will be attacked, chocked and feel being strangled in the spirit. Spirit of fear will cripple me feeling hopeless. In some instances, I will feel having sexual intercourse in dreams. This is what majority of people are going through. Even born again believers.

Many have been sent to mental wards due to demonic possession. Scores of people have been placed on powerful psychic tropic drugs and they become chemically bound zombies. It is high time we start attacking the kingdom of darkness to save many souls.

Most of the time we retreat while we should be demolition the alters of kingdom of darkness.

One-third of Jesus' ministry was operating in casting out demons and teaching His disciples how to free the enslaved captives. Old Testament and New Testament do not ignore the power of witchcraft over people and nations; both Testaments show the only answer to these powers is the Almighty Power God through the name of His Son, Jesus. Being born again means a spiritual rebirth, new creature, the old man is gone. We shouldn't be tormented by spirits suffering attacks. But bold enough to believe the Bible and the ministry of Jesus and set captives free by casting out devils.

This is a major issue that has kept many in bondage. The idea of witchcraft is to control the individual and make them to conform to what you them to do. The principality in the marine kingdom is responsible marriages in spirit. Marriage in spirit is real just as physical marriage is real.

This type of marriage is conjured up in the marine kingdom. The setbacks, poverty and misfortune you encounter in life some of the thing may be the result of spiritual marriage. You can only get this through a revelation. Dreams are also important in our lives in pointing spiritual issues.

Through the grace of God, I was able to break off any spiritual marriage conjured up. These demons would suck your power and finish you up. They will ride with your power to achieve their own agenda. Sex is powerful. It is sacred to God.

The devil uses it to control and destroy the lives of millions. It is painful since many would be ignorant that they are married in spirit. Spiritual marriage is just bad. Marriage are supposed to be natural. You cannot enjoy your life knowing that a creature at night sleeps with you. It is in fact embarrassing.

Programmed to follow devil

The man of God is highly ranked in the kingdom of the devil. He programme the souls of the believers to follow the enemy. We need believers who are grounded in the word of God. And also who are trained enough in the demonology and able to wage warfare with the kingdom of the darkness. I was one of the souls initiated into the kingdom of the darkness summoned by the man of God to work every night.

Barnabas Lekganyane is a principality mention in the book of Ephesians 6:12. I made it a point in my life to immerse myself with the word of God. So I can defeat the kingdom of the darkness especially the marine kingdom because it is one of the dangerous sect of Satan.

The marine kingdom can bless you, and can curse you. But to be blessed you have to sell your soul. The devil doesn't play along and doesn't have freebies. You pay with your life to amass great wealth that would leave you peace less. As Christians we have to be sober and vigilant because they initiate people through dreams. Some people and Christians have joined unknowingly.

Missions impossible from the devil

I was taken to marine kingdom wherein I met men with black gowns. They told me to sleep with women and capture their souls. This is how many men of God receives their powers. It is by sleeping with people; it doesn't matter if they are men or women. Fortunately, I have never even though of doing that. Because I was initiated by the bishop, it wasn't something I wanted. There are so many ranks and jobs one may do in the kingdom of the devil. The only plan is to turn the whole world into worshipping Satan.

I have seen important leaders come to the City under the Sea such as Indians, Asians and Americans. These people were coming from all over the world, from everywhere. I saw very famous influential people; actors and actresses and even saw powerful political personalities in the underwater spirit world. These were people who had sold their souls for positions of power. They had given themselves over to greed and demon possession. They had sold their souls just to sit upon the seats of thrones of world tycoons, barons and kings.

I was more disappointed and displeased seeing bishops, pastors and prophets whom we follow under the marine kingdom spirit world. These is the people who we follow not knowing they are following the devil himself. John 10:10 The enemy comes to steal, kill and destroy. The whole plan of the enemy is to institute his own religion and new of order of living. He is after the souls of God. He is still angry that he was humiliated and thrown out of heaven (Isaiah 14 and Ezekiel 28). He is penetrating every center with his devilish intentions to turn the world into his place of worship.

Underworld (Big productions)

This is the place of demonic habitation. I have seen spirit of ancestors being called up and appearing. The ministers of God will inquire from them about a certain individual for information. These prophets will prophecy correct info but playing along with the familiar spirits. This place I am talking about is filled with captured souls of men and women who work day and night for their capturers. I have seen this underworld kingdom of the ZCC where there a big production where people are working. The branded tea that you drink are manufactured in the underworld.

I saw a lot of things that are hard to explain. I saw people chained, people used for making money - their duties are to work day and night to supply money to their captors. I saw SOME ELITE SECRET SOCIETY MEMBERS who came in to do some sacrifices and would go back to the world with some gifts given to them by the spirits controlling the place. These so called men of God are herbalist. They profess the name of the Lord but deny him with their actions.

The whole plan of the enemy is to bring deception and destruction upon earth. And to cause high level of rebellion to God. The idea is to wipe the name of God and substitute it with his own dealings. In the book of Ezekiel 28 and Isaiah 14 we are told how he defiled his place of worship with his dealings (business). The devil has always been a business man since the beginning of time. He led the numerous angel away from God through dealings. It is the same today, he will give your riches, honor and powers of this world in exchange of your soul.

The church of Jesus Christ is asleep. Many religious leaders are the agent of the enemy and we don't know it. We are just blindly following. It is a shame. We need to be equipped and armed with all spiritual powers of God to diffuse the influence of the kingdom of darkness in churches.

Chapter 19-Nephilim's (Fallen angel)

(Genesis 6: 4) When men began to increase on earth and daughters were born to them, 2the divine beings saw how beautiful the daughters of men were and took wives from among those that pleased them. —3The Lord said, "My breath shall not abide in man forever, since he too is flesh; let the days allowed him be one hundred and twenty years."—4It was then, and later too, that the Nephilim appeared on earth—when the divine beings cohabited with the daughters of men, who bore them offspring. They were the heroes of old, the men of renown.

The second is Numbers 13:32-33, where the Hebrew spies report that they have seen fearsome giants in Canaan: And they spread among the Israelites a bad report about the land they had explored. They said, "The land we explored devours devours those living in it. All the people we saw there are of great size. We saw the Nephilim there (the descendants of Anak come from the Nephilim). We seemed like grasshoppers in our own eyes, and we looked the same to them."

These giants called Nephilim's shoots from the sons of God who descended from heaven to intermarry with women. They were more like hybrid of human, angel and creature. They polluted the whole earth with their evil dealings, killing, murder, stealing and high level of immorality among others.

Noah stood out among the rest of humanity as an example of righteousness and godliness in a world that have completely gone insane with perverse corruption and immorality. The flood swept away these giants and left Noah with his family. The spirit of these fallen angel and Nephilim has been the center of worship for centauries especially in Africa.

The thunder spirits and destruction were see are as the result of these spirits. Oceans, seas, rivers and mountains inhabit these spirits. When someone head to mountains and streams of rivers to worship more or less they put their lives in danger. It has always been a tradition to separate yourself for pray and fasting in segregated places. They are angels disguising themselves as the angel of light. I personally have spent the amount of my time communing in rivers and mountains praying. I can attest that these places are inhabitations of god and goddess. Unfortunately, we as African we have substituted God with these creatures.

I have come with the conclusion that, Barnabas Lekganyane also has more or less substituted the Almighty God with these mountain and river creatures. The mere fact that his headquarters, called Mount Moriah, resides gods, not God of Israel. This came as a revelation from the Almighty God. God Almighty wants to save his children, not only Zionist but Africa as whole for following the detestable traditions of the forefathers who worshipped these beasts. Traditions of men are not gateway to heaven. Only the truth shall set us free. It is high time we take a firm stand on the solid rock affirmed by holy sages of the ancient times.

Psalm 24: 1-2 The is the LORD and the fullness thereof; the world, and they that dwell therein. For he has founded it upon the seas, and established it upon the floods. The seas are filled with mysteries. Elisha did not send Naaman to any river but to a specific river. Naaman would not be healed if he went away to any river of his wishes. He found deliverance and healing from his leprosy condition on Jordan river.

Jordan was not just any river but a portal to the heavenly. This is where Joshua placed stones of pillar. The priest and Levites passed by with the ark of God. This were Elijah was transported to the heavenly. Later on John the Baptist baptizes Jesus Christ on the same water. All I am saying is that, the water belongs to God. But at the same time the devil has perverted it. The kingdom of the devil came the marine kingdom also has its domain under water. This where most of the cult priest, witchdoctors and Sangoma gets their powers.

As much as Jesus Christ opened his spirituality in the river, the enemy is also using the same method. There is power in water. Because the spirit of the Lord was hovering upon the waters before creation. The devil is fighting everything that God has. He always wanted to be like the Most High. Get the gist of these by reading Isaiah 14 and Ezekiel 28. Indian ocean is where the power of Zion Christian Church stanches from. It makes sense, as the leader is the marine priest.

The trademark of every marine priest is the use of water in their service. ZCC predominately uses water as their point of healing and deliverance. India is the home shrine of this mega church. The cow is predominately praised in India as a god. Same as the followers of Zion Christian Church following the cow as their god. This is further heard even in their praises and worships. Everything is attributed to "KGOMO". Pure idolism and paganism.

Daniel 11:36-39 And the king shall do according to his will; and he shall exalt himself, and magnify himself above every god and shall speak marvelous things about the God of gods, and shall prosper till the indignation be accomplished: for that that is determined shall be done. Neither shall he regard the God of his fathers, nor the desire of women, nor regard any god. For he shall magnify himself above all. But in his state shall he honor the God of forces; and a god whom his father's knew not shall he honors with silver and gold and with precious stones, and pleasant things.

This scripture above is about the anti-Christ human who will disregard the ways of his forefathers and indulge himself with the strange gods. The mere fact that Christ is not the central figure in the lives of Zion Christian church Member should be questioned. The most exalted figure is Barnabas Lekganyane. He is centered around the prophecies, songs and worships. He is the day to day messiah of Masione.

Spirit of leviathan is one of the dangerous spirit ever in the sea. God talk time out to detail leviathan in Job 41. From the scripture we see that leviathan is not intimidated by anyone. Who dare to arouse him? He is the king of all pride. The king of all underwater creatures. The leviathan rules in the seas beneath and above. This spirit is very much dangerous because it can be programmed to follow you wherever, whether you relocate or go to overseas it will still follow you.

The fruits of this spirit are; divination, familiar spirits, false manifestations, necromancer, religious spirits, haughty devils, and works of unrighteousness, death and destruction; this is what majority of mega churches in African and beyond worship. This is the spirit that gives out false manifestations, vision and dreams. The church is sleeping on this spirit, mainly because you don't hear much teaching about Leviathan and marine spirit.

I had a revelation from God that the power of ZCC comes from Leviathan, the dragon that is in the sea. This dragon doesn't only reside in the sea beneath but even in the water of the heaven in the second heaven. The philistines used to serve and worship this idol called Dagon. This is the spirit of the water that causes destructions upon earth. Spiritually every now and then, you will see the leader of the church going in and coming out of the water kingdom. He made pact with the devil to serve the kingdom. It is really affecting those who don't know about his dealings.

During the Exodus Moses went head to head with King Pharaoh whose powers came from Nile river since he made a deal with sea monster, Leviathan because he is the king of all monsters in the sea. The Lord God had to divide the sea and destroy the monster to diffuse the powers of King Pharaoh. I will punish leviathan the piercing serpent, even leviathan the crooked serpent, with Your sore, great, and Strong Sword – the Word of God (Isa.27:1). The stony heart of Leviathan was in Pharaoh with miracles he saw but was unable to release the nation of Israel out of his kingdom.

This spirit is at play in prophecies. ZCC prophecies are of divination, necromancer and false manifestation. This spirit is building scales upon the eyes of the believer so that they can never know the truth. Only truth will set you free from all form of bondage and slavery. Clearly anything whereby God is absent is off the prototype of all bondage and slavery. The dangerous spirit of ZCC is a burden unto the believers. This is kundalini spirit at work!

References

Alolo, N. A, African Traditional Development And concepts of Development: Development: A background Paper, Working paper 17-2017

Danam G. 2018, The Sacrifice of The Firstborn in the Hebrew Bible, The University of Sheffield .

De Visser, AJ. The Zion Christian Church .

Miracle Deliverance: World Marine Spirits By DR Pat Holliday.

Hagee, J. 2015. The Three Heaven: Angels, Demons And What lies ahead. Worthy books, Tennessee.

Simon Moripe, Mokhukhu dance, University of Limpopo.

Don't miss out!

Visit the website below and you can sign up to receive emails whenever Thabang Tefo publishes a new book. There's no charge and no obligation.

https://books2read.com/r/B-A-HQQW-WGGGC

BOOKS2READ

Connecting independent readers to independent writers.

Did you love *Occult Church Exposed: My Firsthand Testimony*? Then you should read *Occulthood In Church: My Firsthand Testimony*[1] by Thabang Tefo!

[2]

Are you ready to dive into a gripping and eye-opening read? Look no further than "Occult Hood in Church: My Firsthand Testimony."

Thabang Tefo has firsthand experience with the dark and disturbing practices that occur behind closed doors in some religious institutions. In this compelling memoir, they take you on a journey through their own personal experience with the occult and its presence within the church.

From mysterious rituals to unexplained occurrences, the author bravely recounts their own journey of discovering the unsettling truth about what was really going on within the church they attended. This

---

1. https://books2read.com/u/4j5Zv5

2. https://books2read.com/u/4j5Zv5

book is not only a personal testimony but also a warning to others about the dangers of blindly following religious leaders without question.

With vivid detail and a captivating narrative, "Occult Hood in Church" will have you on the edge of your seat as you discover the shocking reality of what can happen when spirituality is taken to a dangerous extreme. Don't miss out on this powerful and thought-provoking read that is sure to leave you questioning everything you thought you knew about faith and religion

About the Author

Before he started writing Christian books, Johannes got a graduate degree in Film and Television from university of Johannesburg. After that, just to shake things up, he went to equip himself with religious studies, particularly Christianity, just to have knack about the world beyond the curtains of time. And how this body of Christ has transformed millions of people around the world, not neglecting how sadly the movement has been persecuted from time to time. He now writes full time.